Outstretched Arm of the Lord

Alex Ndukwe

Copyright © 2019 Alex Ndukwe

All rights reserved

This book or any portion thereof may not be reproduced or used without the express written permission of the publisher except for the use of brief quotations in a book review

First printing, 2019

Printed in the United States of America

ISBN: 978-1-79474-562-9

Dedication

I dedicate this book to my spiritual children – **Sister Adama Usman, Brother Sheye Samuel, Sister Ebere.** They believed in me and have been a source of encouragement.

Table of Contents

Page

The Arm of The Lord?

Chapter One

Outstretched Arm of the Lord in Action

Children of Israel Delivered from Egypt ...

David defeats Goliath ....

Elijah defeats Prophets of Baal ....

Hebrew boys Survives blast Furnace ....

Jesus Christ an Outstretched Arm of the Lord ....

Saul arrested by Jesus ....

Chapter two

Angelic role in Outstretched Arm of the Lord

What do angels look like? …………………..

What do angels do? ………………………...

Named Angels and Angelic beings …….

The Journey out of Egypt …………………

When Jesus was crucified ..……………….

During Apostolic Age ……………………….

Daniel's encounter with Angels ..………….

Chapter Three

Invoking Outstretched Arm of the Lord

Fasting and Prayer …………………………..

Praise and worship, Thanksgiving ………..

Decree and Declaration …………………….

Chapter Four

Let's take our position

Foreword

I served with Pastor Alex Ndukwe in Kano at the Redeemed Christian Church of God, Solid Rock Area. Then he was working with a bank. He was committed and always doing the work of God without reservation. He was promoted as a zonal pastor as a result of his zeal and goal getting attitudes. This book tells us his experience about the miracle working power of God- The arm of God.

The arm of the Lord delivers from any form of bondages and captivity, perform signs and wonders, assist in defeating your greatest enemy, bring freedom from affliction, bring miraculous, provision, makes a way where there was no way and so on. These effects of the arm of the Lord can be experience in your life if you can pay the prices as stated in this book.

I warmly recommend this book to you knowing that most of your challenges now will be overcome by taking your position as a child of God and follow the instructions in this book carefully. I pray that you will begin to experience miracles, signs and wonders from now in Jesus name.

Pastor Onipede Oludare
PIC, Zone RCCG, jubilee house parish.
Bayelsa State

The Arm of the Lord?

I quite appreciate the questions in our hearts with respect to the above, but God is a spirit and how come the Lord has an arm, this phrase refers to the display of undisputable power of God considering turn of events in the life of men.

Prophet Jerimiah referred to the arm of the Lord in chapter 32 verse 17, 'Ah Lord GOD! behold, thou hast made the heaven and the earth by thy great power and stretched out arm, and there is nothing too hard for thee', it is evident that creation of heaven and earth was an enormous task beyond just spoken word , the Arm was involved when it got to the critical stage of this exercise, his Arm was outstretched.

When Man was created was after heaven and earth had been completed, Genesis 2:7, 'And the LORD God formed man of the dust of the ground and breathed into his nostrils the breath of life; and man became a living soul.' Man was created in his own image and the help mate was created from the rib of the man , Genesis 2:21-22, 'And the

Outstretched Arm of the Lord

LORD God caused a deep sleep to fall upon Adam, and he slept: and he took one of his ribs, and closed up the flesh instead thereof; And the rib, which the LORD God had taken from man, made he a woman, and brought her unto the man.' This was achieved by the outstretched arm of the Lord; it was a surgical operation that was carried out by pulling out the rib from man and this is demonstration of the Lord's power.

This is a proof to show that the Lord has an arm and when it is outstretched then there will be a display of raw power of God and no one can stop or manipulate it. We should not confuse this write up and we should understand the word of God was equally used in creation , Rivers were created , a Garden was also planted and this was the abode of man, Mineral resources was created like gold, bdellium and onyx was also deposited in the ground.

The book describes the O-A-L displayed and what it takes to invoke it and as Christians we need to take our faith serious and be ready to crack bones and stop sucking milk for the rest of our lives and we should not forget that the Keys of David was laid upon the Shoulders of Jesus(Isaiah 22:22), this is dominion and power , this same scripture indicates that Doors opened no man can shut and doors shut no man can open. As children of God , we can lay claims on this inheritance according to Romans 8:17 we are heirs , heirs of God and Joint-heirs with Christ and these keys are technically upon our shoulders.

We need to grow beyond fulfilling all righteousness by just been in church on Sundays , we must ensure powers handed over to us is properly utilized for our benefits and also for others and I must confess that we have not taken our rightful position and this accounts for some ills in our society today, we must be prepared to take charge by the guidance of the holy spirit.

Chapter One

Outstretched Arm of the Lord in Action

'Ah, Lord God! Behold, You have made the heavens and the earth by Your great power and outstretched arm. There is nothing too [a]hard for You.' (Jerimiah 32:17)

The outstretched Arm of the Lord is evident in the old and new testament of the bible and this serves as great hope for the believers and also help to strengthen our faith and remind us that all the covenant made by the almighty will be established in the name of Jesus.

The children of Israel had spent 430 years in the land of Egypt and the Lord promised to deliver them and take them to a Land that flows with milk and honey, this promise was made to Abraham (Gen 15:13-14) and the Lord used Moses to carry out this assignment, Exodus 6:6, "Therefore, say to the Israelites: 'I am the Lord, and I will bring you out from under the yoke of the Egyptians. I will free you from being slaves to them, and I will redeem you with an outstretched arm and with mighty acts of judgment."

Indeed the task was a difficult one, but God was involved and with God nothing will be impossible(Luke1:37) and the strategies were unfolded , the Lord had to harden the heart of pharaoh (Exodus 9:12) and this prevented further dialogue or negotiations with Moses , a hardened heart if filled with destruction and would want to handle all proceedings with force and military might.

Let us not get carried away we can clearly see in the second paragraph as highlighted by the quoted scripture, the Lord promised to redeem the Israelites with an outstretched arm and mighty acts of Judgement, an enormous display of undisputed power , 10 plagues were unleashed in the land and they are as follows:

1) **Water turned to blood** - "Thus says the Lord, 'By this you shall know that I am the Lord: behold, I will strike the water that is in the

Nile with the staff that is in my hand, and it will be turned to blood. The fish that are in the Nile will die, and the Nile will become foul, and the Egyptians will find difficulty in drinking water from the Nile'" (Exodus 7:17-18).

2) **Plague of Frogs** - "And the Lord spoke to Moses, 'Go to Pharaoh and say to him, "Thus says the Lord: 'Let My people go, that they may serve Me. But if you refuse to let them go, behold, I will smite all your territory with frogs. So the river shall bring forth frogs abundantly, which shall go up and come into your house, into your bedroom, on your bed, into the houses of your servants, on your people, into your ovens, and into your kneading bowls. And the frogs shall come up on you, on your people, and on all your servants'"'" (Exodus 8:1-4).

3) **Plague of Lice** - "So the Lord said to Moses, 'Say to Aaron, "Stretch out your rod, and strike the dust of the land, so that it may become lice throughout all the land of Egypt."' And they did so. For Aaron stretched out his hand with his rod and struck the dust of the earth, and it became lice on man and beast. All the dust of the land became lice throughout all the land of Egypt" (Exodus 8:16-17).

4) **Plague of Flies** - "And the Lord said to Moses, 'Rise early in the morning and stand before Pharaoh as he comes out to the water. Then say to him, "Thus says the Lord: 'Let My people go, that they may serve Me. Or else, if you will not let My people go, behold, I will send swarms of flies on you and your servants, on your people and into your houses. The houses of the Egyptians shall be full of swarms of flies, and the ground on which they stand. And in that day I will set apart the land of Goshen, in which My

people dwell, that no swarms of flies shall be there, in order that you may know that I am the Lord in the midst of the land'"'" (Exodus 8:20-22).

5) **Plague of Livestock** - "Then the Lord said to Moses, 'Go in to Pharaoh and tell him, "Thus says the Lord God of the Hebrews: 'Let My people go, that they may serve Me. For if you refuse to let them go, and still hold them, behold, the hand of the Lord will be on your cattle in the field, on the horses, on the donkeys, on the camels, on the oxen, and on the sheep—a very severe pestilence. And the Lord will make a difference between the livestock of Israel and the livestock of Egypt'"'" (Exodus 9:1-4).

6) **Plague of boils** - "So the Lord said to Moses and Aaron, 'Take for yourselves handfuls of ashes from a furnace, and let Moses scatter it toward the heavens in the sight of

Pharaoh. And it will become fine dust in all the land of Egypt, and it will cause boils that break out in sores on man and beast throughout all the land of Egypt'" (Exodus 9:8-9).

7) **Plague of hail** - "Then the Lord said to Moses, 'Stretch out your hand toward heaven, that there may be hail in all the land of Egypt—on man, on beast, and on every herb of the field, throughout the land of Egypt.' And Moses stretched out his rod toward heaven; and the Lord sent thunder and hail, and fire darted to the ground. And the Lord rained hail on the land of Egypt" (Exodus 9:22-23).

8) **Plague of Locust** - "...if you refuse to let My people go, behold, tomorrow I will bring locusts into your territory. And they shall cover the face of the earth, so that no one

will be able to see the earth; and they shall eat the residue of what is left, which remains to you from the hail, and they shall eat every tree which grows up for you out of the field" (Exodus 10:4-5).

9) **Plague of darkness** - "Then the Lord said to Moses, 'Stretch out your hand toward heaven, that there may be darkness over the land of Egypt, darkness which may even be felt.' So Moses stretched out his hand toward heaven, and there was thick darkness in all the land of Egypt three days" (Exodus 10:21-22).

10) **Death of Firstborn** - "Then Moses said, 'Thus says the Lord: "About midnight I will go out into the midst of Egypt; and all the firstborn in the land of Egypt shall die, from the firstborn of Pharaoh who sits on his throne, even to the firstborn of the female servant who is behind the hand mill, and all the firstborn of the animals. Then there shall be

a great cry throughout all the land of Egypt, such as was not like it before, nor shall be like it again. But against none of the children of Israel shall a dog move its tongue, against man or beast, that you may know that the Lord does make a difference between the Egyptians and Israel"'" (Exodus 11:4-7).

This plague brought calamity in the Land of Egypt and Pharaoh's heart became more hardened and would not let the children of Israel to go, Moses received more instruction from the Lord with respect to the sacrifice that should be carried out and feast of the Passover. The children of Israel had to proceed out of Egypt to the wilderness via the Red Sea , Pharaoh would not let go since his heart was still hardened and was prepared for war. The Lord was with the children of Israel and no one can be against them (Romans 8:31).

The Lord provided Navigation for the children of Isreal (Exodus 14:1-3), the Lord further hardened the heart of pharaoh and his army went after them, each time you notice the Lord instructing Moses to stretch his rod and this serves as a connection that will invoke the power of God and we need to appreciate this fact.

When they got to the red sea , the Lord instructed that Moses should stretch his rod towards the sea (Exodus 14:16), the Lord caused an east wind and this caused the sea to go back all that night, and made the sea dry land, and the waters were divided., the children of Israel moved across on the dry land and the pharaoh's horsemen and chariots went after them.

After the children of Israel had crossed over, the Lord instructed Moses to stretch his rod towards the sea and the water came together, the Egyptians were destroyed and their dead bodies found at the shore of the sea. The children of Isreal gained their freedom as promised by the almighty.

Let us look at another display of the outstretched Arm of the Lord in the book of 1samuel 17, David had to confront Goliath the philistine champion. Goliath was described in verse 4, 9 feet 9 inches which is equivalent to six cubits and a span. We might not have David's height but his description in 1 Samuel 16:12. "Now he was ruddy (he possibly had reddish-hair, and a dark physically healthy complexion) and had beautiful eyes (striking features) and was handsome (good looking)."

It's assumed he is of average height. How could he opt to face such a giant and most people assumed that he wants to commit suicide, Saul gave his support, but he felt how could this young man face this champion. Let us look at 1 Samuel 17:45, 'Then said David to the Philistine, Thou comest to me with a sword, and with a spear, and with a shield: but I come to thee in **the name of the LORD** of hosts, the God of the armies of Israel, whom thou hast defied. He went in the name of the Lord, the stave and five stones were just symbolic, this could not have been the reason for his victory because the outstretched arm of the Lord was the main reason for the success.

The philistine could not comprehend why such a small statured man would face a man like him and he said in verse 43, 'And the Philistine said unto David, Am I a dog, that thou comest to me with staves? And the Philistine cursed David by his gods.

David's stave and stones invoked the raw power of God over the philistine , this made it very easy for him to defeat him , verse 49-50 gives us a brief account of how victory was attained, 'And David put his hand in his bag, and took thence a stone, and slang it, and smote the Philistine in his forehead, that the stone sunk into his forehead; and he fell upon his face to the earth. So, David prevailed over the Philistine with a sling and with a stone, and smote the Philistine, and slew him; but there was no sword in the hand of David. He entered Jerusalem with the head of goliath.

Elijah Defeat the Prophets of Baal

There was famine in Samaria , prophets of God in the Land became endangered species , the governor Obadiah had to hide 100 prophets in a cave secretly so as to spare their lives , at this time the people had turned away from God and they were worshiping Baal which contravened the law. Ahab had accused Elijah as one of those causing problems in the Land.

Elijah had to look for how to reconcile his people with God and he had to carry out a test with the god of Baal, the prophets of Baal were 450 against Elijah the prophet of the most high. Details of the contest , 1Kings 18:23-24 , 'Let them therefore give us two bullocks; and let them choose one bullock for themselves, and cut it in pieces, and lay it on wood, and put no fire under: and I will dress the other bullock, and lay it on wood, and put no fire under: And call ye on the name of your gods, and I will call on the name of the LORD: and the God that answereth by fire, let him be God. And all the people answered and said, It is well spoken'

The bullocks was dressed and cut and put on the wood and they called on their god and nothing happened for the whole day and Elijah mocked them , 1Kings 18: 27 , 'And it came to pass at noon, that Elijah mocked them, and said, Cry aloud: for he is a god; either he is talking, or he is pursuing, or he is in a journey, or peradventure he sleepeth, and must be awaked.' Nothing happened.

It was Elijah's turn to call on his own God , he prayed a prayer in 1Kings 18:37 , 'Hear me, O LORD, hear me, that this people may know that thou art the LORD God, and that thou hast turned their heart back again' The prayer invoked the outstretched arm of the Lord and then the fire of the LORD fell, and consumed the burnt sacrifice, and the wood, and the stones, and the dust, and licked up the water that was in the trench. And when all the people saw it, they fell on their faces: and they said, The LORD, he is the God; the LORD, he is the God. Elijah went after the prophet of baal and slew them.

This proofs that one with God is majority in any circumstance , for the Land to be healed the people must turn back to God , the servant of God informed Ahab to go up and eat and drink for there is an abundance of rain , he went to mount Carmel and prayed until the heavens opened and rain fell.

Three Hebrew boys Survived the blast Furnace

King Nebuchadnezzar of Babylon made a graven image and made it mandatory that the everyone in the kingdom should bow down and worship the it. Shadrach, Meshach, and Abednego refused to adhere to this instruction and the information reached the king and these boys were summoned , Daniel 3:14-16 , 'Nebuchadnezzar spake and said unto them, Is it true, O Shadrach, Meshach, and

Abednego, do not ye serve my gods, nor worship the golden image which I have set up? Now if ye be ready that at what time ye hear the sound of the cornet, flute, harp, sackbut, psaltery, and dulcimer, and all kinds of music, ye fall down and worship the image which I have made; well: but if ye worship not, ye shall be cast the same hour into the midst of a burning fiery furnace; and who is that God that shall deliver you out of my hands? Shadrach, Meshach, and Abednego answered and said to the king, O Nebuchadnezzar, we are not careful to answer thee in this matter.

These Hebrew boys are fully aware that God is a consuming fire , they put their trust in him , instructions from the King was that the temperature of the blast furnace be increased 7 times, normal temperature should be 2300 Degrees , recommended temperature became 16100 Degrees , scientifically no human can survive such and environments , even the men that set it up died in the process before these boys were thrown into the furnace.

The Outstretched arm of the Lord will always make a remarkable difference and these boys were thrown into the furnace under the supervision of Nebuchadnezzar , Daniel 3: 24-25 , 'Then Nebuchadnezzar the king was astonied, and rose up in haste, and spake, and said unto his counsellors, Did not we cast three men bound into the midst of the fire? They answered and said unto the king, True, O king. He answered and said, Lo, I see four men loose, walking amid the fire, and they have no hurt; and the form of the fourth is like the Son of God.

Almighty God provided insulation for these boys and the fire had no effect on them and they came out of the furnace unhurt and the Lord proved that 'There's no God Like me' and the King made a decree in Daniel 3:29-30 , 'Therefore I make a decree, That every people, nation, and language, which speak anything amiss against the God of Shadrach, Meshach, and Abednego, shall be cut in pieces, and their houses shall be made a dunghill: because there is no other God that can deliver after this sort. Then the king promoted Shadrach, Meshach, and Abednego, in the province of Babylon.

Jesus Christ an Outstretched Arm of the Lord

Interestingly the Arm of God has been in operation since creation and the Almighty sent his son , a physical manifestation of the Father and we should not forget that John 1:14 says that the word became flesh and dwelt in our midst , the journey of salvation came alive. The name could be described as powerful and undisputable when there is trouble. Philippians 2:10-11 , 'That at the name of Jesus every knee should bow, of things in heaven, and things in earth, and things under the earth; And that every tongue should confess that Jesus Christ is Lord, to the glory of God the Father.'

Prophet Isaiah had predicted his birth in Isaiah 9:6 and in Isaiah 22:22 described his powers , the Keys of David will be upon his shoulder , these keys stand for dominion and power over situations, challenges and circumstances, Any door he decides to open no man can shut and any door he shuts no man can open.

During his earthly ministry lots of miracles, signs and wonders were executed by the master that people might believe and the outstretched arm of the Lord was very evident. The mad man of garderer had legions on demon residing inside of him , this man lived in a cemetery and in John 5:8 the master decreed , 'For he said unto him, Come out of the man, thou unclean spirit' , it came to pass and the man behaved normal. What of the man with infirmities for 38 years at the pool of Bethesda , Jesus came in contact with him and asked a simple question, will you be made whole and he began to tell stories, no one would help him when there is turbulence in the pool and in John 5:8 , 'Jesus saith unto him, Rise, take up thy bed, and walk.' , immediately the man was made whole.

Even cases that looked irredeemable , the man that was dead for 4 days and already stinking , the relatives of the dead complained he arrived late and he reminded them that he is resurrection and life, in John 11: 43, 'And when he thus had spoken, he cried with a loud voice, Lazarus, come forth.' The dead man came forth and he ask them to loose him and let him go. Outstretched Arm of God dwelt in our midst during his earthly ministry and he charged his disciples in John 14:12 , 'Truly, truly, I tell you, whoever believes in Me will also do the works that I am doing. He will do even greater things than these, because I am going to the Father.'

After his ascension the scripture in the preceding paragraph came to pass and the key word is 'whoever believes in me' , anyone that accepts Jesus as Lord and personal saviour , lives holy becomes a joint-heir with Christ as indicated in Romans 8:37 , this implies that the outstretched arm of the Lord is also deposited on every believer by adoption.

During the Apostolic age it came to pass , notable miracles were executed by the apostles , At the beautiful gates a crippled beggar begging for alms was healed by peter , this man looked at his direction for money and peter in Acts 3:6 , 'Then Peter said, Silver and gold have I none; but such as I have give I thee: In the name of Jesus Christ of Nazareth rise up and walk.' His ankle received strength and peter dragged him up and he began to leap and afterwards started to walk. An hopeless situation was recorded in Joppa , Acts 9:36-7 , a widow full of good works called Dorcas had died and sorrow filled up the environment and news got to them that peter was in Joppa and they sent for him, the servant of God knelt down and prayed , in Acts 9:40 ,

'..........and turning him to the body said, Tabitha, arise. And she opened her eyes: and when she saw Peter, she sat up.'

Apostolic Age was full of persecution and arrests, peter was thrown into prison and the church prayed earnestly for him , suddenly light shinned into the prison, angel of the Lord opened the doors , his bounds were loosed (Acts 12:5-7).

Paul and Silas were thrown into a maximum security prison and they were bound in chains , they prayed and sang praises , there was an earthquake and the prison doors were opened and the chains binding them were loose , this was a raw display of the outstretched arm of the Lord in action , this was during the apostolic age. The power of God was intense then, today is a different ball game.

Saul Arrested by Jesus

Saul was the chief prosecutor of preachers , he had powers to arrest , torture and to Kill, Acts 7:58 , 'And cast him out of the city, and stoned him: and the witnesses laid down their clothes at a young man's feet, whose name was Saul. A young Pharisee consumed by zeal, pursued a program to purge Jerusalem — and every Jewish community — of any trace of Jesus' teaching or influence. Single-minded in his dedica-tion to the task, he went about "breathing threats and murder against the disciples of the Lord"

This marked the beginning of the first coordinated, systematic persecution of the Church. Most of the disciples fled Jerusalem and went into hiding. Some took refuge among Israel's most notorious apostates, in Samaria, where the Phari-sees and other religious authorities would be unlikely to ven-ture. Only the Apostles stayed behind in the holy city.

Saul was not a docile minion, blindly carrying out orders issued by higher authorities. He was the most active agent of persecution, moving it forward and prosecuting the matter himself. Not content with a local police action, he "went to the high priest and asked him for letters to the synagogues at Damascus, so that if he found any belonging to the Way, men or women, he might bring them bound to Jerusalem"(Acts 9:1-2).

On his way to Damascus, Jesus arrested him and in Acts 9:3-4, the encounter that he had was revealed, " And as he journeyed, he came near Damascus: and suddenly there shined round about him a light from heaven: And he fell to the earth, and heard a voice saying unto him, Saul, Saul, why persecutest thou me?" Apparently was confused and in the process, he lost his sight and confirmed the voice that was speaking to him, Acts 9:5, "And he said, Who art thou, Lord? And the Lord said, I am Jesus whom thou persecutest: it is hard for thee to kick against the pricks."

This is to proof to you that the outstretched power of the Lord can bring a sinner to Christ with an encounter and we need to appreciate it , this story shows that there is no one God cannot use for his service , let us conclude this interesting story. Saul had no sight for 3 days and fasted for this period. The men that travelled with him were all confused as the heard the voice and saw no man.

God commissioned Ananias , And the Lord said unto him, Arise, and go into the street which is called Straight, and enquire in the house of Judas for one called Saul, of Tarsus: for, behold, he prayeth, And hath seen in a vision a man named Ananias coming in, and putting his hand on him, that he might receive his sight.(11-12). The disciple was afraid considering the evil this man had done to the saints in Jerusalem. He had to proceed on the assignment and in verse 17-18 , "And Ananias went his way, and entered into the house; and putting his hands on him said, Brother Saul, the Lord, even Jesus, that appeared unto thee in the way as thou camest, hath sent me, that thou mightest receive thy sight, and be filled with the Holy Ghost. And immediately there fell from his eyes as it had been scales: and he received sight forthwith, and arose, and was baptized."

The persecutor started to preach the gospel of Jesus Christ , can you see how powerful the outstretched arm of the Lord is , arrested Saul of Tarsus and he became a preacher of the word of God. Most people reacted in verse 21, "But all that heard him were amazed, and said; Is not this he that destroyed them which called on this name in Jerusalem, and came hither for that intent, that he might bring them bound unto the chief priests?"

In this chapter we have seen that the outstretched arm of the Lord can do the following:

(a) **Deliverance** – the power can deliver us from bondage, shackles of the enemy, contrary powers of the enemy. Isaiah 59:16 , Isaiah 62:5, Acts 16:25 , Acts 12:5-8

(b) **Salvation** – Like the story of Saul of tarsus, we don't need to force anyone to Christ rather we need to pray that the fellow has an encounter with God and this will make the work easy. I was discussing with my mother she asked me a question, I have just started a new ministry and it's evident I embark on vigorous evangelism on Saturday , that means you will mobilize more members and I corrected her, I told her that such an assignment is to preach to the unsaved so that they might come to the kingdom of light and one should not force them to a particular church, the holy spirit will take it up from there. 1 Corinthians 3:6, 'I have planted, Apollos watered; but God gave the increase.' , it's only God that can bring increase , not out efforts alone. What of the incidence that happened in Acts 16:25 , the prison doors were opened by the outstretched power of the Lord and the keeper of the prison gave his life to Jesus, what an encounter, Acts 16:30,"And brought them out, and said, Sirs, what must I do to be saved?" , the keeper of the prison and his entire household were saved. Isaiah 52:10, Isaiah 53:1, Galatians 4:4-5, Ephesians 1:10-11

(c) **Signs and wonders** – The raw power of God is displayed; miracles would come alive because of the power of God destroys all yokes of the enemy. Sorrow would be turned to Joy, Lack to abundance, anxiety to peace like a river, bareness to fruitfulness, sickness to good health etc. Luke 5:6, John 5:8, Acts 9:40, Acts 3:6, John 11:44, Mark 5:8

(d) **Undisputable power of God** – we discussed the conquest between Elijah and 450 prophets of Baal, fire of the Lord consumed the sacrifice. As children of God we have power to destroy every power of the enemy (Luke 10:19). 2 Kings 13:21, Acts 9:17-18.

Chapter two

Angelic Role in Outstretched Arm of the Lord

"But the prince of the kingdom of Persia withstood me one and twenty days: but, lo, Michael, one of the chief princes, came to help me; and I remained there with the kings of Persia."

Angels and angelic, heavenly beings created 'spirit' beings of God: Colossians 1:15-18, Hebrews 1:14, Psalm 8:4-5. Made before creation of the earth had part in making it: Job 38:3-7, Psalm 148:1-6, they don't belong to either the male or female gender. Often referred to as messengers or intermediary are in different categories, let us deal with this before proceeding with the biblical evidences. The types of angels are as follows:

- Archangel(s)
- Seraphim or Seraphs
- Cherubim or Cherubs
- The Four Living Creatures
- Lucifer, Satan, The Devil
- Fallen Angels, Evil Spirits, Demons

What Do Angels Look Like?

'Ordinary' Angels. No full description, but something special: Judges 13:6, Revelation 10:1, Look like 'normal' people. 'tall young men with shining faces and wearing white simple robes': Matthew 28:2-7 , Mark 16:1-7 , Luke 24:1-8 , my friend pastor owolabi saw one while we had a programme in Kano, according to him this fellow looked very simple and discussed with him, then he was in charge of organising transportation for brethren that attend the breakthrough service, suddenly the man disappeared.

What Do Angels Do?

God's Messengers: Luke 2:8-18, Matthew 28:2-7, Acts 10:1-8 (chief messenger, Gabriel)

Encouragers: Judges 6:12, Acts 12:7, Acts 23:23-25

God's Holy Warriors: Revelation 12:7-9, Ezekiel 28:11-19

Watching History Unfold: 1 Corinthians 4:9, Luke 15:7, Daniel 4:13-17
Praising & Worshipping God: Revelation 7:11-12, Revelation 5:11-12, Psalms 148

'Guardian Angels' protecting & Guiding people on behalf of God: 1 Kings 19:4-8, Acts 5:17-20. Nothing about 'personal' angels in the Bible. There for all Christians: Hebrews 1:14, Psalm 34:7

Angelic protection for Children: Matthew 18:10
Following Death: Luke 16:19-31

Named Angels and Other Angelic Beings

Michael - means 'Who is like God?'. Great Warrior: Revelation 12:7. Guard on the nation of Israel: Daniel 12:1 Michael is the only Archangel in the Bible: Jude 9. Gabriel - means 'God's Hero', God's messenger: Daniel 8:15-17, Luke 1:8-20, Luke 1:26-38

Archangels – In the Bible only Michael names as Archangel. Jewish trad, seven: Revelation 8:2. They, along with the angels, are guardians of people and all things physical. But don't call on them to help you personally; archangels respond best when dealing with matters involving all humankind. They are the first order of angels that appear only in human form. As such, they function among us as pioneers for change in the form of explorers, philosophers, and human rights leaders.

Seraphim - means "burning ones" or nobles. Also called 'ones of love'. Six wings (two to fly). Role to constantly glorify and praise God: Isaiah 6:1-7 Holy x3 means 'perfectly holy'. These are the angels who are closest to God. They encircle his throne and emit an intense fiery light representing his love. Seraphim are considered "fiery serpents" and not even the other divine beings may look at them. There are only four of them and each has four faces and six wings. When they come to Earth, they leave their serpent appearance behind, preferring tall, thin, clean-cut human embodiments.

Cherubim – Guardians. Surround the throne of God. Two wings, other description beyond understanding! These angels are the keepers of celestial records and hold the knowledge of God. They are sent to Earth with great tasks, such as expelling humankind from the Garden of Eden. Ancient art depicts cherubim as sphinx-like, winged creatures with human faces, not the fat babies with wings that now grace greeting cards and book covers. Ophaniel, Rikbiel, and Zophiel are cherubim, as was Satan before his fall to evil. Ezekiel 1, Ezekiel 10 Guarded Eden after the fall: Genesis 3:24 Associated with 'wheels': Ezekiel 10:9-13 Also known as 'throne angels': Psalm 99:1

On ark of the covenant and in the temple: Exodus 25:17-22, 1 Kings 6:23-28

Four Living Creatures – may be Seraphim, Cherubim or something different! Revelation 4:6-10

Satan, Lucifer, The Devil & Demons, Evil Spirits

Angelic Rebellion during creation. Lucifer fell and took about a third of angels with him: Revelation 12:7-9, Revelation 12:4

Lucifer (Morning Star) / Satan was the head angel: Isaiah 14:12-15 / Ezekiel 28:11-19 Satan (meaning Adversary or Enemy) is called: a dragon, someone who 'leads the world astray', the accuser, the 'lord of filth', a liar and the father of lies, a roaring lion looking for someone to devour, the 'prince of this world' and the 'god of this age'.

Demons, Evil Spirits, Unclean Spirits

Followed Satan and were cast out of Heaven. They know/knew Jesus and his power: Mark 1:22-28, Mark 5:1-16 Want us to turn away from God and will try every trick in the book! Work in the Occult. 1 John 4:1-3, Revelation 16:13-14

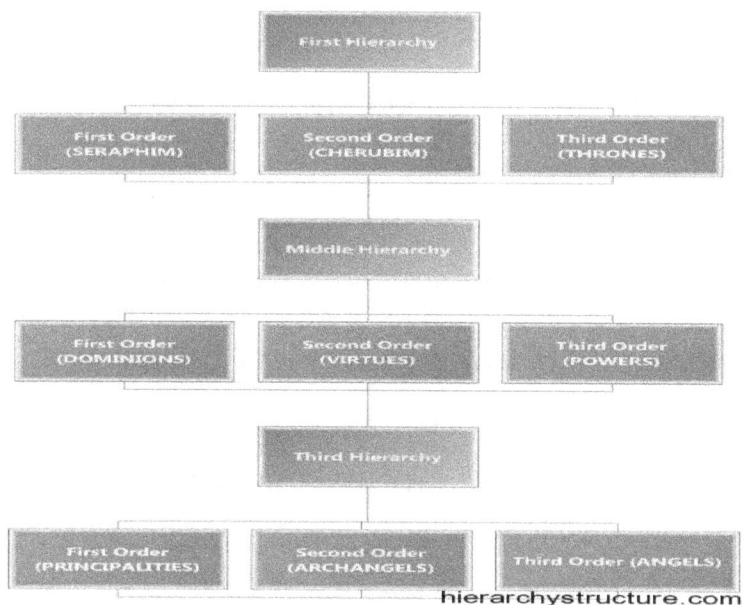

The Journey out of Egypt

The angel of the Lord rendered support , the account is in exodus 14:19 , 'The angel of God who was going before the Israelite army moved and went behind them; and the pillar of cloud moved from in front of them and took its place behind them.' The pillar of cloud was a form of protection and later became a source of light in darkness when it went behind. It came between the army of Egypt and the army of Israel. And so, the cloud was there with the darkness, and it lit up the night; one did not come near the other all night. (verse 20)

As the Egyptian army proceeded towards the Red sea, they saw the Lord in the pillar of fire and cloud looked down upon them and they became afraid and thrown into confusion. The wheel of their chariot was clogged and turned with difficulty and Egyptian army concluded that it's better to flee for God is fighting for them. This action impeded their movement and they couldn't catchup with the Israelites while they are crossing over the red sea.

Though another set of Egyptian armies was close to them and the Lord tossed them into the sea and the Lord ask Moses to stretch his rod over the sea and it closed, and the Egyptian army was destroyed and none of them survived. Angels were on assignment during this operation,

Israelites did not lift a finger to fight and victory was sure.

When Jesus was crucified

Jesus had just eaten his last supper with his disciples and knew that after his time of prayer in the garden, one of them (Judas Iscariot) would betray him and governmental authorities would arrest him and sentence him to die by crucifixion for claiming to be a king. Although Jesus meant that he was king of the universe (God), some officials in the Roman empire (which governed the area) were afraid that Jesus intended to become a king politically, overthrowing the government in the process.

A spiritual battle between good and evil was also raging on, with both holy angels and fallen angels trying to influence the outcome of Jesus' mission. Jesus said his mission was to save the world from sin by sacrificing himself on the cross to make it possible for sinful people to connect to a holy God through him.

Reflecting on all of that and anticipating the pain he would have to endure in body, mind, and spirit on the cross, Jesus went through an intense spiritual battle in the garden. He struggled with the temptation to save himself rather than following through with his original plan to die on the cross. So, Archangel Chamuel, the angel of peaceful relationships, came from heaven to encourage Jesus to move forward with his plan so that the Creator and his creation could experience peaceful relationships with each other, despite sin.

Matthew 26:53 says the angels were standing on the precipice of Heaven, awaiting the order from God to deliver His Son. But that order never came. Jesus said in Matthew 26:53 to His accusers, "Do you think that I cannot appeal to My Father, and He will at once put at My disposal more than twelve legions of angels?" But Jesus never made that request, because He understood His purpose for coming. Jesus said,

"The Son of Man did not come to be served, but to serve, and to give His life a ransom for many" (Mark 10:45). Christ came to make the only acceptable sacrifice for our sins, and the angels witnessed the whole episode.

But it did not stop there. Three days later, the angels were also eyewitnesses to Christ's resurrection from the dead. On that Easter Sunday morning, a violent earthquake occurred. The grave was heavily fortified because there was believe that the disciples would come and steal the body. An angel came and rolled the stone away and sat upon that stone, and the women came to find the Lord. Just picture that angel, sitting on that stone, with his arms probably crossed as if to say, "So much for the power of the grave!" The women inquired where the Lord was, then the angel said, "Do not be afraid; for I know that you are looking for Jesus who has been crucified. He is not here, for He has risen, just as He said" (Matthew 28:5-6).

Weeks later, when the Lord in His resurrected body was about to ascend into Heaven, the Bible says the angels were not only in Heaven watching the event, but two angels were also on earth watching the event. As Jesus ascended into Heaven, the crowd was gazing into the sky. And those angels said to the crowd, "Men of Galilee, why do you stand looking into the sky? This Jesus, who has been taken up from you into heaven, will come in just the same way as you have watched Him go into heaven" (Acts 1:11).

During Apostolic Age

Angels played prominent roles during the apostolic age, during this period there was persecution of disciples of Jesus Christ and it was a taboo to preach the gospel and most of them were tortured and thrown into prison. In the book of Acts 12:5-7, Peter was thrown into prison and the Church prayed for him and suddenly light shinned into the prison, an angel had come to rescue him. The supernatural abilities of this angel are as follows:

- He could suddenly materialize in a secure area.
- He could move through solid walls.
- He could put trained soldiers into a deep sleep.
- He could cause locks to open and solid chains to fall off.
- He could cause Peter to move from the innermost part of the prison to the exit without being seen.
- He could cause iron gates to open.
- He could disappear into the thin air.

Peter came out of the prison because of the help of an angel. Same incident occurred in Acts 16:25, though the bible did not mention any angel , Paul and silas prayed an sang praises and suddenly there was an earthquake and the prison doors were opened and their bands were loosed , An angel was responsible for this action , this was to proof to the keeper of the prison that God can deliver and existence of the power of God, keeper had no choice but to make inquiries on what he needs to do to be saved.

Stephen referred to angels four times in his sermon in Acts 7, and we're told that his face became like the face of an angel.

In Acts 8:26, an angel of the Lord appeared to Philip and told him to go down to the road to Gaza to meet the Ethiopian eunuch. He saw him in a chariot, had to join him in the chariot and discovered he was reading aloud Isaiah 53:7, 'He was oppressed, and he was afflicted, yet he opened not his mouth: he is brought as a lamb to the slaughter, and as a sheep before her shearers is dumb, so he openeth not his mouth.' And Philip enquired from him do you understand what you are reading and he said No, he had to explain and used the opportunity to witness and on their way they saw a river and the eunuch asked Philip what will it take me to be baptised and he said only if you belief and he was baptised, the Lord caught up Philip and he vanished from the water and the Ethiopian eunuch rejoiced.

In Acts 10, an angel appeared to a centurion in Caesarea named Cornelius and told him to send for Peter. Acts 10:3-5, 'He saw in a vision evidently about the ninth hour of the day an angel of God coming into him, and saying unto him, Cornelius. And when he looked on him, he was afraid, and said, what is it, Lord? And he said unto him, Thy prayers and thine alms are come up for a memorial before God. And now send men to Joppa, and call for one Simon, whose surname is Peter:'' He got the description of his house and the spirit of God told him three men seek after you please follow them. The purpose was for him to be under his ministration and baptised with the holy ghost. The purpose was achieved while he was under his ministration.

Daniel's Encounter with Angels

Daniel 6 gives us his first encounter with angels , it was a taboo to pray to other Gods , while in Babylon in faced the direction of Jerusalem and prayed and the news reached the King and an instruction is reeled out that he should be thrown into the Lion's den.

The king went after 3 days and discovered Daniel was unhurt and he responded in Daniel 6:22 , '22 My God hath sent his angel, and hath shut the lions' mouths, that they have not hurt me: forasmuch as before him innocency was found in me; and also before thee, O king, have I done no hurt' and the king responded in verse 23 , 'Then was the king exceeding glad for him, and commanded that they should take Daniel up out of the den. So, Daniel was taken up out of the den, and no manner of hurt was found upon him, because he believed in his God. The king now decreed that the accusers and their families be thrown into the den and they were destroyed by the lions. King dairus decreed , 'I make a decree,

That in every dominion of my kingdom men tremble and fear before the God of Daniel: for he is the living God, and stedfast for ever, and his kingdom that which shall not be destroyed, and his dominion shall be even unto the end.'

In Daniel 10, Daniel had a dream and trusted God for interpretation and an angel was sent to meet him and was withheld for twenty-one days by prince of Persia and Arc angel Michael was sent to rescue him (Daniel 10:13).

You can imagine the delay and frustration that Daniel had to experience before the Angel arrived. Many bible scholars had imagined why an angel should be sent to interpret his vision, it shows how important the revelation is to the entire people and most importantly the holy ghost had not been sent to the world at this period , Angels played prominent roles in delivering messages, the Lord had provided the answers through him.

Brethren Angels are still in operation and I pray we will have an encounter someday in the name of Jesus , every child of God that is living right has a guardian angel and don't forget some of us say 'something tells me this is not right' , one might ask what could this be?, it's definitely the guardian angel giving you a clue. I remember vividly last year I went to see my account officer and interestingly she made an assertion that made me have goose pimple while she spoke, in her words, 'I see some things following you and it just spoke to me that you are very honest and any money disbursed you will pay back' and she asked me are you a pastor? And I responded YES.

It was a testimony and I am not qualified to access any facility but she will see what she can do, I returned to my office and in another 40 minutes she called to inform me that she has arranged a facility of 2million through a customer and I should come and issue my cheque for the repayment with a post-dated cheque and I was shocked to the marrow.

Chapter Three

Invoking Outstretched Arm of the Lord

Follow peace with all men, and holiness, without which no man shall see the Lord:'
Hebrew 12:14

We are aware of the basic attributes of a child of God, unfortunately mix multitudes have joined the work force and has risen to become pastors, ministers and so on but we must be conscious of the fact that titles will not take us anywhere. Fear of God spiced with Christ like behaviour will take us to the promise land as we embark on our journey to cracking bones and proving that we are representative or ambassador of the most high , when we are confronted with situations we can take our rightful place.

Invoking outstretched arm of the Lord reveals the supreme powers that is available for our use but it doesn't come easy but a price must be paid by the children of God in question don't forget as our Daddy in the Lord Pastor Adeoye would say

'Nothing goes for Nothing' , how do we invoke the Arm of the Lord , undisputed power of God in Action.

I know answers are been expected from the submissions from the second paragraph and I can confidently reveal that it would come alive with **Fasting, Prayer, Praise and Worship, Thanksgiving.** The reaction from different quarters is Afterall we have been doing all these and why cant we invoke that arm, I want to ask a simple question, 'what is in your heart?' it's vital no matter the kind of faith you exhibit and we must be conscious of this(I refer you to my book on **What's in your heart** please check it out). What is the intensity of these activities highlighted because that would invoke the power if all other conditions that are referred to as prerequisites , peter made an assertion in Acts 10:34-35 while pouring encomium on Cornelius before his ministrations and outpouring of the holy spirit, 'Then Peter opened his mouth, and said, Of a truth I perceive that God is no respecter of persons: But in every nation he that feareth him, and worketh righteousness, is accepted with him'

What of when we intend to invoke the arm corporately? We must be united without any iota of strive or hatred, the bible refers to it as one Accord in Acts 2:1. We must be bold and exercise Authority given to us by the almighty.

<u>Fasting and Prayer</u>

The full potential of the Spirit manifested in Christ after a time of fasting, solitude, and prayer. He was a perfect model for us because of His obedience to the Spirit of God and giving Him full control of His life. Our bodies have a way of dictating to us what it wants. When we fast, we serve notice to our bodies that our spirit is in charge and that our bodies are to be obedient to the Holy Spirit's dictates, not the other way around.

In 2 Corinthians 11:27, Paul said, "I have labored and toiled and have often gone without sleep; I have known hunger and thirst and have often gone without food." The words "gone without food" should be translated that Paul had "often fasted." Just previously he wrote that he involuntarily had known hunger and thirst, but also voluntarily fasted from the food that he had available. The King James Version translates the same passage: In weariness and painfulness, in watchings often, in hunger and thirst, in fastings often, in cold and nakedness (2 Corinthians 11:27).

If Paul was in a lifestyle of prayer and fasting often, and God used him so powerfully, we need to realize that this same power is available to us today. Perhaps the amount of prayer and fasting that Paul engaged in was the very thing that resulted in the great grace that was upon his life. Yes, God had a plan for Paul. The Lord answers when faith is expressed. Paul had a zealous faith and would not let God go. In one place he wrote: But he said to me, "My grace is sufficient for you, for my power is made perfect in weakness." Therefore I will boast all the more gladly about my weaknesses, so that Christ's power may rest on me. That is why, for Christ's sake, I delight in weaknesses, in insults, in hardships, in persecutions, in difficulties. For when I am weak, then I am strong (2 Corinthians 12:9-10).

Paul's testimony was that he found a secret—the weakness of his own strength brought the power of God upon him. He said he delighted in being weak so that Christ's power may rest upon him. One thing is sure; we need the power of God to be at work in the Church of the 21st century. It will take men and women who are dedicated to labor with God's energy at work in them and not the strength of our abilities apart from God's enablement. In another place, Paul writes: To this end I labor, struggling with all his energy, which so powerfully works in me (Colossians 1:29).

It is Christ in us, the hope of glory that must do the works of the kingdom. When a man or woman seeks, through prayer and fasting, for God's Spirit to have the reins of one's life, then God can get the glory by doing His work through us. Heaven forbid that the Church should seek for the glory that is due only to Christ. That's why Paul could say to the church in Rome: "I know that when I come to you, I will come in the full measure of the blessing of Christ" (Romans 15:29). He had learned that the Spirit would work powerfully through him as he served the Lord through fasting and prayer. He fully expected that he would come with the Spirit's power.

Great measure of power is eminent when we our spirit is in tune there is bound to be connection with the Lord and heavenly forces , this brings the arm of the Lord into existence when required and wonderful works becomes eminent, people around will marvel but not knowing that lots of efforts had been put in place. Apostle Paul could invoke the power of the Lord because of his making fasting and prayer a lifestyle. Miracles done by Paul are recorded in Acts 14:10, Acts 16:18, Acts 19:11-12, Acts 20:10-12, Acts 28:8 etc. There is no issue that cannot be resolved. We need to activate and invoke the power of God; this makes a huge difference in our lives.

We need to grow up and ensure that this exercise is not seen as a burden but the right attitude for our connection to the Almighty , we need to subdue our flesh so as to ensure that the spirit has an upper hand and as Christians we ensure we always live in the spirit.

Population of Christians is over 2 billion all over the world but the Pentecostals is just less than10% , this should not bee an issue if we can submit ourselves to this exercise we can change the world and reshape the turn of events , I recall how difficult it is for some of us to fast and pray and my friend pays money to prayer contractor to help him fast , this is not a good one as I advised him to stop that , the Key of the house of David was laid upon the shoulder of Jesus and any door he shuts no man can open and any door he opens no man can shut(Isaiah 22:22) and Romans 8:17 indicates we are heirs of God and Joint heirs with Christ , this implies that the Key of David is on our shoulders and how can we put this dominion and power into active use that will invoke the undisputable power of God it's by prayer and fasting spiced with faith , there is no magic in this and the Candid advise is we must fall in line and the Lord will help us in Jesus name.

I have a testimony during the fasting of 2017 then I was still manning a parish at the redeemed Christian church of God, we were already 15 days into the exercise and I had a challenge retrieving the money my former employers took from me , I want to be as polite as possible and I wont mention the name of the bank , the amount was 1million Naira which was used to carry out perfection of Legal mortgage on my mortgage facility.

I sent several emails to Group Head-HR and he claimed the money had been utilized, Flesh asked me to engage a lawyer which I did and the man started to make unnecessary demands because he had to exhume the C of O file at ministry of Land , the third attempt to collect money from me I told him to give me a little time and I went to our parish alter, prayed a simple prayer and I asked

God to intervene , and within 10 minutes the word came from the holy spirit 'send an email to the Group Managing Director' , I should be polite and the mail must be on top of all the mails I have been sending to Group Head-HR , should put all the Executive Directors in copy.

Immediately I left the church I rushed to the office and I followed the instruction and this was on a Monday morning, on Wednesday I received a call from the same Group Head-HR , He apologised that the Bank Lawyer confirmed that the perfection was not done due to insecurity in Kano , I will be credited as soon as possible and Friday afternoon my phone vibrated and I check and found out my account was credited with the sum of 1million naira. Can you see the power of Fasting and prayer? And I avoided excess charges from my lawyer and cost of Legal proceedings.

Another testimony, I was still manning a Church a Redeemed Christian Church of God and we desired to buy a land since our yearly rent was =N=6million Naira per annum and we discovered a Land measuring 3,000 Square meters valued at =N=15 million Naira and we negotiated it to =N=8million Naira and we approached our Regional Pastor and got the sum of =N=5million Naira and a shortfall of =N=3million Naira and incidentally we had just finished the second half fasting in July for 30 days, our spiritual batteries were full and I went before the Lord at home and I told God there is no how we can raise the shortfall since my people are always complaining when it comes to issue of bringing money, I cried 'Lord help me' and the Holy Ghost gave me instruction to invite the Land owner to the church after the workers meeting and 3 names of ministers that should attend the meeting was also given to me and one of them should open the floor and indicate that what we have is only =N=5million for full and final, I will take it up from there.

Meeting commenced 5 minutes to Sunday school and Deacon Okpala opened the floor and the woman took a deep breath, she looked up and down , the office was tensed but already I know the Lord had taken care of the matter and the woman said , 'I have given churches Land free and Pastor Ndukwe what your team has presented is very difficult but no problem because of the work of God I accept =N=5million as full and final , please let me endorse the documents , note that the church will bear the cost of the commission to the agent which is 10%' , this generated another argument and I had to inform them not to spoil our fruitful discussion, we will sort it out by his grace, this meeting stretched into the service, I had to inform the Head usher to handle the message and the deliberations ended 15 minutes to 11, I was so excited and our deacon was already rounding up and I took the microphone from him and I prayed a prayer of thanksgiving for what the Lord had done and I announced to the Church, 'We have processed the Land' and rejoicing was in the air. This happened in first week of August just after we concluded the second half fasting.

Brethren I want you to understand that we can change situation of things in Nigeria if only we can come together forgetting our denominations and doctrines, be in one-accord and go before the Lord we are bound to see changes we never anticipated and the Lord will heal our Land.

Praise and Worship, Thanksgiving

Have you observed during the earthly ministry of Jesus he always gave thanks to God before executing miracles and this usually occurred when it seems very hopeless like when he raised Lazarus from dead, he gave thanks. You can now imagine what will happen when you do this continually.

When Fasting and prayer fails then it's time to praise God, you are making an attempt to Access his courts where the Lord is seated, the psalmist says that you enter his gates with thanksgiving which is a valid visa for you to proceed to his courts with praise(Psalm 100:4-5) and when this happens you touch the throne of grace and the angels will have to review your case file and bring it before the Lord and the implication is instant miracles.

One of our senior pastors in Redeemed Christian Church of God , during the doctrinal teaching in Kano gave this testimony, it happened at a parish in Lagos and he witnessed it, A worker slumped and died , the workers meeting was about to commence and the pastor instructed that the body be deposited in his office and after the meeting he will attend to the case, there was pandemonium in the air , the workers meeting continued and afterwards he assembled the prayer warriors and it was time to pray for the dead and they prayed for 30 minuets and nothing happened , the holy spirit instructed they praise God and they started to praise God and within 15 minutes the brother that was dead sneezed and he got up and there was rejoicing in the air.

There is power when you spend quality time praising God, a day before I had been depressed and in pain , I struggled to sleep and by 2am I started to praise God instead of my normal prayers , I praised God for Long and suddenly I fell into a trance, 'I saw Jesus and a short video clip where I saw my former church administrator and myself we were in a gathering and suddenly because he spotted me, he left the place. I recall he was the one that came up with unfounded allegations against me that led to my removal, I knew already that the Lord needed me for another assignment and there's nothing I could do then, it dawned on me that I need to call him and ask him to forgive me since I had forgiven him last year, I had to call him this morning and I felt peace in my heart. When I called him, he was surprised and he said, 'you have not done anything to me' and I told him all the same please forgive me. I checked my time piece it was 5:49am, meaning I praised God for about 3 hours 49 minutes.

There is power in praising God and my encounter this morning taught me a lesson and I have decided to praise God at least one hour per day for the rest of my life. Pastor Adeboye mentioned praising God during his visit to throne room recently and I learnt from it, I had an encounter when I decided not to pray but praise God for 3 hours.

Praising God as a catalyst has the tendencies of invoking the arm of the Lord, this implies that this activity has the power of speeding up the rate of miracles after spending quality time fasting and prayer. The psalmist says in psalm 50 that God does not need food from us , he owns the entire world and the fulness thereof , cattle's on a thousand hills , beast in the forest , birds in the Air and all he needs from us is thanksgiving and we pay our vows , when we call upon him on a day of trouble, he will attend to us and I pray we have this understanding that God inhibits the praises of his people(psalm 22:3) , one of the major reasons he created us is that we praise him and when we fail to offer praises he can replace us with stones, this will not be our portion in Jesus name.

Decree and Declaration

As a child of God one question is very important; how do you exercise authority? It's either you issue a Decree, or you make declarations. These words are not the same, Decree – This is when you issue a command & Declaration is to make clear, explain, interpret. Decrees create and make changes in the Spiritual and Physical Realm. Scripture is a powerful force that creates change in both the physical and spiritual world when spoken. As you decree God's word and will, the awesome power of the Holy Spirit is released to bring it to pass. This forum is divided into two outlines (1) Decree (2) Declaration, Mathew 16:19 – 'And I will give unto thee the keys of the kingdom of heaven: and whatsoever thou shalt bind on earth shall be bound in heaven: and whatsoever thou shalt loose on earth shall be loosed in heaven.', Mathew 18:18, this scriptures indicates action to be taken by a child of God on the path of righteousness, this can be done by decrees.

(1) Decree – Have you bothered to find out who has the power to make decrees, (a) **Almighty God** (b) **A Child of God**

(a) **Almighty God** –

decrees of God are declarations or pronouncements that He has made in working out His plan in the various ages. The Bible says that God causes all things to work together for good. Romans 8:28, Also we have obtained an inheritance, having been predestined according to his purpose who works all things after the counsel of His will- Ephesians 1:11, According to the eternal purpose which he accomplished in Christ Jesus our Lord - Ephesians 3:11. The decrees of God extend to His creation of the universe, His plan of salvation for humankind, and His providence over all things. There Are a Number of General Statements About the Decrees The Scripture contains several general statements about the decrees of God. Isaiah 14:26,27, Isaiah

46:9,10 , Daniel 4:35 , Psalm 119:89-91, 1 Corinthians 15:23 ,There are several practical benefits that can be derived from understanding God's decrees.

First, there is confidence that what God has decreed will come to pass. What God says will happen; will indeed happen. This also brings humility to the believer. For the unbeliever the decrees warn them of judgment to come. Finally, the decrees bring a genuine hope to believers. Consequently, it is important to understand the things that God has decreed for humanity and for the universe.

2) **As a child of God:**

Decree and Declaration as a child of God. Isaiah 22:22 says 'And the key of the house David will I lay upon his shoulder: so he shall open, and none shall shut: and he shall shut and none shall open. Whom are you? A child of God or a certified Child of God, Don't forget Romans 8:17 , 'And if children, then heirs; heirs of God, and joint-heirs with Christ; if so be that we suffer with him, that we may be also glorified together.' Certified child of God is that child of God that is approved unto God – 2 Timothy 2:15, this child of God has the word on his or her fingertips and ready to release it when required. As joint heirs of God the keys are also upon our shoulders and we can make a decree and heaven will put a seal on it and no body can stop you. When you make a decree is when you make authoritative statement that can transform things around you and challenging situation. You can make decrees with the word of God. Someone oppressed or in bondage, you can decree, I stand upon the word, Luke 10:19, every contrary power binding my sister be destroyed because all powers have been given to me to destroy every power of the enemy in the name of Jesus. Jesus made several decrees, the man with infirmities for 38 years, John 5:8 ,'Then Jesus told him, "Get up, pick up your mat, and walk."

And peter performed a similar miracle at the beautiful gate , Acts 3:6 , 'Then Peter said, Silver and gold have I none; but such as I have give I thee: In the name of Jesus Christ of Nazareth rise up and walk.' , you notice he decreed in the name of Jesus , Philippians 2:10-11, the name is above every name. Let us look at declaration, this can be used to claim the promises of God unto our lives for example, Deuteronomy 14:12, Lord open your treasures unto me and I shall not borrow but lend to nations in the name of Jesus. This is an example of declaration, what of one that is afraid of death, Psalm 118:17, I will not die, but I will live and proclaim what the LORD has done in Jesus name. The bible is full of diverse promises, you can declare these promises and it will come to fulfilment. You cannot know the promises except you study the bible and extract these promises.

The enemy make incarnations which Yoruba's call it and Igbo's offor and a horn of a sheep with some red cloth tied around it and this should make us battle ready because no one knows the day of battle, One afternoon I was at palm groove bus top on my way from school and an incident occurred , a young man insulted a middle aged man and suddenly this man made an incantation and commanded this boy to remove his clothes , this boy was hypnotized and he removed his clothes and people gathered. A child of God appeared and he made a decree , 'There no relationship between light and darkness' in the name of Jesus name above all names put on your clothes and the boy put on his clothes and people were rejoicing, power exchanged hands.

When the power has been drawn down , decrees are required to bring it into fulfilment and release a powerful bullet with the word of God , Job 22:28 comes into play , these words become established and light shines upon our way, let us strive to be a certified child of God cracking bones.

Chapter Four

Let's take our position

'If my people, which are called by my name, shall humble themselves, and pray, and seek my face, and turn from their wicked ways; then will I hear from heaven, and will forgive their sin, and will heal their land.''

Our society has been ravaged by some evils and I would agree some are signs of the end times but as Christians we should not keep quite and assume that we cannot change the situation prayerfuly, I'm sorry I have to make reference to my former church Redeemed Christian Church of God, it's my root , we had suffered a lot from the hands of kidnappers and one holy ghost service Pastor Adeboye raised a prayer against kidnappers and I remember that we all prayed and within some days the kingpin evans was arrested , this slowed down their activities and no one could arrest him, let us imagine every denomination put our nation in prayer by now things would have been better.

Outstretched Arm of the Lord

We can recount Elijah and the 450 prophet of baal (1 Kings 18:37-39) , the fifty soldiers sent to arrest this man of God three times and he called fire from above( ) and fire fell and consumed these soldiers and the sacrifice. A man of God called fire, can't our fathers in the Lord call on fire to consume boko haram and the heards men, lots of innocent lives are already lost and we must take our position as children of the most high.

The chief of Army staff , Lt. General Tukur Buratai organized a conference on Spiritual warfare and he came under heavy criticism in the media, yes he cannot be wrong if our spiritual leaders cannot suggest this and even go as far as organising a conference on this , we should understand that God can use anyone to remind us that we need to seek his face in some battles that we cannot win after spending millions of dollars buying weapons.

Mr Buratai, a lieutenant general, said Nigeria and the world at large was grappling with the harsh reality of restiveness mostly shrouded in religious, economic and political undertones. "These tendencies have caused disorder and wanton destruction of lives and property of many innocent citizens who have continued to look unto the government for solace. The COAS described the theme, "The Non-Kinetic Strength in the face of Armed Banditry and other Security Challenges: The Role of the Military Chaplains", as very relevant in this battle. He further noted that the choice of the Northwest for the event meant they were in tandem with the efforts of the government in quelling the teeming security challenges of banditry in the region. He called for more collaboration between the Directorates of Civil Military Affairs (DCMA) and the three Religious Directorates in the efforts to contain the security challenges. (Premium times, 'Why we adopted spiritual warfare to counter Boko Haram – Buratai', October 23, 2019 , page 1)

The boko haram would not engage in such a battle and rely only on weapons, they also have some spirituality involved and this accounts for reasons this war has refused to come to an end and North East remains ravaged. While we continue to invest in this war we should also don't forget that we can call on God to help us in this war and nothing stops us from calling fire from above to destroy them or better still trust God to set confusion in their midst and they destroy themselves, no one has made this attempt , let us make an attempt first let's see if God will not help us and end this war.

Don't forget Jehoshaphat got a hint that 3 nations were coming against Judea, the first step he took was to declare fasting and prayer and the word came from Nathan the prophet, 'Go to the war praising my name' , most people felt this is a suicidal bid and they followed the instructions religiously and suddenly the three nations came against themselves and the Jehoshaphat and his men inherited the spoils, the battle was eventually won.

Wars that remains difficult let's tackle it spiritually and I believe all will be well in the name of Jesus victory will be our portion once we are ready to take our position.

Our Religious Leaders have a role to play in this direction, though I agree we have intercessors groups in Nigeria praying and once in a while they organize prayer meetings that are considered interdenominational in nature but the last edition took place 2 years ago and we need to make it an annual event if really we are serious to fight spiritually.

There are other battles we can fight spiritually, economic sabotage like the smuggling of products that are illegal through our boarders, looting of public funds etc. we can fight the saboteurs prayerfully and heaven will pay attention to these prayers and put a seal on it.

We are inhabitants of this great country and should not negate spirituality in reshaping our destiny and more so we should not forget that we can only enjoy peace if we cry to the Lord to calm all our storms , we need to pray fervently for it to come alive and bearing in mind God is the creator of heaven and earth , Jerimiah 32:17 , 27 , Luke 1:37 should be on our lips because he is the God of All flesh , Nothing shall be hard for him to accomplish , with God nothing shall be impossible. If valleys of dry bones can become a strong mighty army in the land of Israel, then there is nothing God cannot do in Nigeria.

Our interest should not only be the state of decay in our dear nation but also, we should visualize what the prayer of the righteous can do and the Lord will help all of us in our nation, God bless our Nation Nigeria.

Outstretched Arm of the Lord